Antique Piano

& Other Sour Notes

Barbara Etlin

DecoOwlPress

TORONTO

Copyright © 2014 by Barbara Etlin.

All rights reserved. No part of this publication may be reproduced, distributed or transmitted in any form or by any means, including photocopying, recording, or other electronic or mechanical methods, without the prior written permission of the publisher, except for brief quotations in reviews.

info@decoowlpress.com

"The Seven Maids Form a Union," "Refrigerator Magnet Collage," and "Clock Watcher" were originally published in *Danse Macabre* in October 2010.
"Dear Round-Headed Kid," "Renovating the Past," "Embroidery," and "Ode to the Homepage Muse" were originally published in *Free Zone Quarterly* between 1997 and 2002.
"Embroidery" won the Virtual Photo Gallery Contest, 2002. "Pig" won the Pig Haiku Contest, 2013.

This is a work of fiction. Names, characters, places, and incidents are a product of the author's imagination. Locales and public names are sometimes used for atmospheric purposes. Any resemblance to actual people, living or dead, or to businesses, companies, events, institutions, or locales is completely coincidental.

Cover Design by Kevin Slattery
Proofreading by Linda M. Au
Book Layout © 2013 BookDesignTemplates.com

Antique Piano & Other Sour Notes/ Barbara Etlin. – First edition
ISBN 978-0-9921258-0-6

Contents

CHAPTER 1: Paperback Writer 1
The Seven Maids Form a Union 3
Ode to the Homepage Muse 4
Mercury Lament 6
Ode to Elmer 7
Seasonal Excuses 9
CHAPTER 2: Moondance 11
Too Many Moons 13
Mystery Man 14
Etiquette for Astronauts 15
CHAPTER 3: You and I 17
Misdialled 19
Embroidery 21
Romantic 22
Heartbreak Kid 23
Why I Said Yes 24
CHAPTER 4: Lucy in the Sky with Diamonds ... 25
Refrigerator Magnet Collage 27
Clock Watcher 29
Fool's Gold 30
The Queen's Own 32
CHAPTER 5: Japanese Mode 35
Revenge 37
Pig 38
Plastered 39
Meditation on Calculation 40
CHAPTER 6: Don't Rain on My Parade 41

Meltdown 43
Something Is Rotten 44
Remind Me 46
Of Cabbages and Kale 47
Highway 401 Revisited 48
Renovating the Past 50
CHAPTER 7: Parodies and Grace Note 51
Favourite Things 53
Antique Piano 54
Stevie Wonder's Sunshine 56
CHAPTER 8: Pet Sounds 59
Dear Round-Headed Kid 61
To My Neighbour's Cat 63
Believe You're a Puppy 65
and Other Advice from Echo ....
Acknowledgements 67

For Michael, Airwolf Theme.

In memory of Frances Etlin, Sophisticated Lady.
Mom, my name is finally on the cover. Yes, in big letters.

"Oh, that baby grand will go up the stairs. No problem!"

– Piano Mover

CHAPTER ONE
PAPERBACK WRITER

The Seven Maids Form a Union

MEMO

TO: Mr. Lewis Carroll
FROM: The Seven Maids' Union
RE: Your poem, "The Walrus and The Carpenter,"
              in your novel, "Through the Looking Glass"

Just because we've worked so long
Without a cent in pay,
Don't think that we will go along
With that for one more day.

As you will note, our work has stopped.
We're powerless no more.
So if you want your ocean mopped
Up from the ocean floor,

You owe us over a hundred years
Of retroactive wages,
Plus overtime—Oh, stop those tears!—
Or we'll desert your pages.

Ode to the Homepage Muse

Pagemaker, Pagemaker,
make me a page.
Find me a home
that's all the rage.

Use graphic software
and HTML
to earn me a writer's wage.

For Vern, please,
make it descriptive.
For Helen,
make it witty as hell.
For me, well,
I wouldn't squawk if it
made all my scribbling
sell and sell.

Pagemaker, Pagemaker,
don't make it grey.
Don't make it pink.
Just make it pay.

Pagemaker, Pagemaker,
hurry up please.

Design me a page.

Link me a link.

Leave out the ads.

Don't let it blink.

And make it a great home page.

Mercury Lament

When Mercury's in retrograde
it always foils me. It will raid
creativity and cause cascade
of brain. And all the plans I've made
to write will go askew. I wade
through computer repairs,
Blue Screen of Death.

My fancy new mouse doesn't roar
and I don't know what good it's for.
(It sure won't move the cursor.)
I feel as though I'm slogging through
a prehistoric swamp of…glue.
(I notice that my rhymes become
progressively worser.)

Though Skype is free I'd gladly trade
for working speakers that don't fade
when Mercury's in retrograde.

ODE TO ELMER

O, Elmer,
elegant Edsel of typewriters!
How I miss your
creative word coinage,
your mysterious and elusive
case ofhic cough s wh ich would
disappear when the doctor came
and r eapp ea r aft e r he'd left.

What joyous times we had
in windowless fluorescence
behind the fortress walls
where none could detect
the difference between thinking and sleeping.

O, Elmer,
who now cruelly torments your keys?
Can she appreciate
your wicked sense of humour?
Does she remember
to put your pyjamas on at night?
Does your life seem
mechanical
humdrum
accurate
now?

Can anyone else
turn you on
as I once did?

Seasonal Excuses

I can't submit my short story in **July**.
Vacation season starts now.

I can't submit my short story in **August**.
August is the slowest month of the year. No one is in the office.

I can't submit my short story in **September**.
The kids are starting back to school and chaos will ensue.

I can't submit my short story in **October**.
I need the entire month to prepare Halloween costumes.

I can't submit my short story in **November**.
I'll be busy doing NaNoWriMo instead of submitting.

I can't submit my short story in **December**.
Everyone knows no one in publishing does any work between mid-November and New Year's Day. They're partying or hung over, if they're in the office at all.

I **can** submit my short story in **January**.
The editors will be back from their six-week-long vacation and will be rested. However, my manuscript will be lost in the huge slush pile that collects between mid-November and January.

I can't submit my short story in **February**.
Winter is too depressing. I'm going to hibernate.

I can't submit my short story in **March**.
The kids will be on March break and chaos will ensue.

I can't submit my short story in **April**.
April is the cruellest month.
(Don't ask me why. Ask T.S. Eliot.)

I **can** submit my short story in **May** and **June**,
so I'd better hurry and write something.

CHAPTER TWO
MOONDANCE

Too Many Moons

Emperor: It's quality work. And there are simply too many notes, that's all. Just cut a few and it will be perfect.
Mozart: Which few did you have in mind, Majesty?
(Sir Peter Shaffer, *Amadeus*)

"Eschew the moon!
Extoll the radish!"

Poetic advice
that makes me saddish.

Mystery Man

One small step can seem like almost nothing,
a quarter million miles for three to fly,
as we held our breaths to watch that first landing.

Four billion hopes—a planet's wondering
reflected in the mirror in the sky—
is one small step away from almost nothing.

Buzz followed you, while Mike was orbiting.
How could your tiny step not make us cry
as we breathlessly watched that first landing?

The media frenzy you found stifling,
a leap to fame that you would soon decry.
One small step can seem like almost nothing.

Who is this man? The press is suffocating.
Cocooned within your silence you just sigh,
and hope news will eclipse the first landing.

Mystery Man, no moon songs do you sing.
Can astronauts be brave, but also shy?
One small step that changes everything
at once. We exhale, hope for safe landing.

Etiquette for Astronauts

Do you think you can just come
here,

plant your flag
on my cratered surface,

play a few rounds of golf
(without replacing your divots),

and then leave me?

You didn't even
take out the garbage.

Earth Man,
you may think you're a big hero.

But don't come back
until you've learned some manners.

CHAPTER THREE
YOU AND I

MISDIALLED

beep

Hi, Jason. It's me.
I know you're probably busy
with your work and all.
Or maybe you're out.

pause

Okay.
I know you said not to call you again.
But I think you should know
that I'm fine with us
being just friends
and I don't understand why
you think we can't talk anymore.
You said, "No commitment,"
and I was fine with that.
Remember?

So I'm really not being
demanding
or anything,
and it's none of my business
where you are at 10:30
on a weeknight,

so busy you can't even answer your phone,
but I really would appreciate
a phone call
now and then.
Okay?

Call me.

Okay?

beep

EMBROIDERY

Pile your words
ceiling-high, if you dare.
Your excuses are embroidered clichés.
Humiliating.
Useless.

Some day you may wish to take back
your insults,
your lies,
your ghosted heart.

But you can't reupholster
a marriage hard as
a sleazy motel mattress,

even if you needlepoint "I'm sorry"
a hundred times
in rainbow colours
on a pillow you can throw at the wall
when you receive
the Decree Absolute.

Romantic

picnic at twilight
secluded cove
on the beach

I spread a soft blanket
over the sand
and wait for you
to twist the corkscrew

we clink crystal glasses
and sip sparkling wine
feast on fresh raspberries
dipped in dark chocolate
licking it off
fingers and lips

waves crescendo
bodies entwine

your cell phone rings

why didn't you tell me
you're married
to your job

HEARTBREAK KID

Ephemeral promises of my midnight caller,
Daring me to stay on the line.

Fireworks dazzle against the coal-black sky
But fizzle under dawn's brightening lines.

Intrigue's a game. You thrive on hunt and chase.
Your trench coat and fedora have classic lines.

Whispered dreams you wouldn't dare tell her.
She only wants to make you toe the line.

Diamonds refract light because they are
Meticulously cut along precise lines.

Are you the stuff that dreams are made of,
Or just a cartoon hero, inked-in lines?

I've chased around your bases long enough.
I won't play second base. I've drawn the line.

Why I Said Yes

Dental plans
come and go,

talking of Michelangelo.

But parking spots
are forever.

CHAPTER FOUR
Lucy in the Sky with Diamonds

Refrigerator Magnet Collage

Spock raises one eyebrow
at the company he must endure.

Bogie, in his white dinner jacket,
invites Spock to a game of chess,
but first Bogie must learn
how to play on that three-level board.

"Think you can beat me, Vulcan?
Used to play in Central Park
during the Depression,
a dollar a game.
I'm good. I'm very good."

"Fascinating," Spock says.
"But I refuse to eat meat."

"Huh?" Bogie says.

"See that owl-shaped piece of paper
with the grocery list?
It says *hamburger*."

"I like hamburger," Bogie says.
"Ordered it every day
for lunch at Romanoff's.

I once got in there
without wearing a tie.
Mike didn't like it
but he couldn't kick me out."

"Humans are so illogical," says Spock.
He brings out the chess board and sighs,
one eyebrow still raised.

Clock Watcher

the eyes of Dr. T.J. Eckleburg
watch the rosewood clock

time melting in a Dali painting
that needs fresh batteries

and T.J. is eternally young
although he wears glasses
his blue eyes
will never get crow's feet

running backward
as fast as you can
won't make you any younger

and blue eyes
in yellow glasses
hanging on the wall
laugh at the valley of ashes

when the rosewood clock
runs out of time
it will gaze enviously at

the eyes of Dr. T.J. Eckleburg

fool's gold

we ate maraschino cherries
while waiting for dessert in Sausalito
but your words twisted around your tongue

on the Golden Gate Bridge
headlights glared
in regular white rows
like a new set of false teeth

the waitress pointed
her toe at the bridge
eager to show off her ballet technique
and she forgot to bring us the long spoons
(never on sundae)

how many fools
came here searching for gold

the Year of the Dragon is golden
once every sixty years
but the Golden Gate Bridge never was
and never will be

it's just fool's gold
a rusty orange
as artificial as
the toxic colour of
maraschino cherries

The Queen's Own

I hadn't been to Casa Loma
in several years.
So I was surprised
to find myself there last night
standing in a long line
outside the stone gate.

Casa Loma,
the house on the hill,
is a Gothic folly
built by a businessman
with an ego too big
for an ordinary house.

Although Sir Henry Pellatt
belonged to the Queen's Own Rifles
he thought he was
a big shot in other ways.

His dreams were bigger than his wallet
and he couldn't pay the taxes on Casa Loma.

So I stood in line
and it took forever
for the elderly woman
in front of me
to move up.
Impatient, I said,
"Beep, beep."

The old lady turned around
to see who was so impertinent
and I was shocked to see
she was Queen Elizabeth.

Was she checking out
Canadian real estate

or was I pushing my way
through life
forgetting my manners
to accommodate
dreams and ego
that knew no boundaries?

I guess I just don't know my place.

Wherever it is,
it's certainly not
the Queen's Own.

CHAPTER FIVE
Japanese Mode

REVENGE

evil black squirrel
voracious tulip muncher—
dinner for my owl

PIG

fry it for bacon
roast it for a fine luau—
kosher it is not

Plastered

invented new sport
figure skating on carpet—
cast as her trophy

Meditation on Calculation

forgive me if I
don't see the point of counting
up to seventeen

meaning is eclipsed
by too much arithmetic—
Basho's frog would croak

CHAPTER SIX
Don't Rain on My Parade

MELTDOWN

Water, water everywhere.
It's spilling on the floor.
When cold is hot
you know you've got
to hurry to the store.

Alas, poor fridge,
you've had the biscuit.
And now I'll have to
dump the brisket.

Something Is Rotten

Life is too short
for flossing three times a day.

No, I still haven't given up
my addiction to Diet Pepsi.

My lack of fresh cavities
is not an invitation
for you to renovate my mouth.

Although you say,
Dentistry is not an exact science
(but if I botch it the first time
I'll give a 10% discount on the second try),

I still believe
temporary or permanent paralysis
is unacceptable.

Unwaivered,
unwavering,
I leave,
with two unanswered questions.

What *exactly* did you learn
in four years of dentistry school
if it wasn't *science*?

And what makes you think
I'd ever come back
for a second try?

REMIND ME

Today. After dinner.

SHE: I just remembered that this morning you told me to remind you to do something today.

HE: Oh, yeah. What was it?

SHE: I can't remember what it was, but I just wanted you to know that I remembered to remind you.

HE: Thanks a lot.

Of Cabbages and Kale

The thought of cabbage makes me quail
And long to drown in Carlsberg Ale.

Repeated stabs of gaseous pain
Make cabbages my diet bane.

Although they've lots of Vitamin K
I'd rather get it some other way.

Highway 401 Revisited

Well, Kingston town, it's got three pens.
Took pictures of them with my zoom lens:
Fountain, Ballpoint and the Quill.
Been penned up so long, it's got me ill.
(I've got it wrong? What's that you say?
They're Kingston, Millhaven and Collins Bay?)
Clear to see, my vacation's done.
Gotta get back to Highway 401.

The road it cuts through walls of granite.
Tank's full of gas, and so I gun it.
Zippin' on past Cataraqui.
Trippin' on past Napanee.
Slower traffic keep to the right.
Never could say no to a fight.
Pedal to the metal, vacation's done.
Avoiding the speed traps on Highway 401.

I've heard tell that some folks say
This road's named Macdonald-Cartier Freeway.
Ain't no one gonna tell me that's its name.
Been Four-Oh-One so long, it's a losing game.
Slower traffic keep to the right.
This could be a real long night
If I don't get back soon to have some fun.
Don't wanna be stuck in traffic on Highway 401.

Now the afternoon sun's been shining in my eyes,
And the cop with the radar gun surely tells lies.
"Don't argue with him. You'll be here all night."
Slower traffic keep to the right.
Don't tell me those roadside dead birds are just flukes.
Darlington Provincial Park is where they keep the nukes.
Canada goose cloud in a burning blue sky
Points west, towards home, and so do I.

Renovating the Past

he's ambitious

so he climbs the ladder
without looking down
without missing a step

using a wide paintbrush
he splashes whitewash over everything
destroying evidence

and if a colourful under layer
wearing a jaunty beret
is overly assertive

it won't trip him up

that's what
dry cleaners
and breath mints
are for

CHAPTER SEVEN
Parodies and Grace Note

Favourite Things

Bogie and Betty and Stevie and Dylan,
Writing a novel that makes me a killin',
Santana's magic on his guitar strings,
These are a few of my favourite things.

Coffee and cookies and new books and wi-fi,
Chocolate and Holland and owls and sci-fi,
Agents with contracts that make my heart sing,
These are a few of my favourite things.

Snow ploughs that clear all the snow from my driveway,
Dogs who know French and play shortstop when we play,
Red tulips pushing through snow 'cause it's spring,
These are a few of my favourite things.

When the mail comes,
When it doesn't,
When I'm feeling sad,
I simply remember my favourite things
And then I don't feel so bad.

Antique Piano

What do you do with an antique piano,
What do you do with an antique piano,
What do you do with an antique piano
When you need to move it?

Schlep it out and crowd your condo.
Schlep it out and crowd your condo.
Schlep it out and crowd your condo.
"Where'll we put our furniture?"

Call technician, get appraisal.
Call technician, get appraisal.
Call technician, get appraisal.
"Sell it as an antique."

Email store and send some pictures.
Email store and send some pictures.
Email store and send some pictures.
"Sorry, not our market."

Pay big bucks to get refurbished.
Pay big bucks to get refurbished.
Pay big bucks to get refurbished.
"It's not worth your money."

Put in storage 'til it's rotten.
Put in storage 'til it's rotten.
Put in storage 'til it's rotten.
No one wants the piano.

Heave it out the upstairs window!
Heave it out the upstairs window!
Heave it out the upstairs window!
Ornately carved firewood.

What do you do with an antique piano,
What do you do with an antique piano,
What do you do with an antique piano
When you need to move it?

Stevie Wonder's Sunshine

expectant hush
hands on the keyboard

reggae beat
You Are the
Sunshine of My Life

dreadlocks
    swinging
he rocks
    to the rhythm
harmonica-playing
    human metronome

seventeen thousand people
dancing in the aisles
clapping so hard
our palms are on fire
don't go yet
one more
encore

and we see Stevie feels it
radiating the stadium
and we feel Stevie sees it
through his dark glasses

sunshine of
reflected
love

CHAPTER EIGHT
Pet Sounds

Dear Round-Headed Kid

Although your services as
Dinner Provider and Chocolate Chip Cookie Supplier
have been adequate,
I must protest the lack of amenities
in my outdoor shelter.

I hereby propose a solution
which I hope you will deem satisfactory.

If you will allow me to reside
within your indoor shelter,
I promise to go along with
your delusion that I am only a dog.

When others are present,
I will bark and wag my tail.
However, I draw the line at
doing demeaning things such as dog tricks.

In exchange, I expect the following concessions:
1. A laptop computer on which I can write my novel.
2. Use of your bed. You may share it with me.
3. Only the finest quality, home-baked cookies.

My solicitor will notify you when the contract is ready.

Yours truly,
Snoopy Beagle

(in memory of Charles Schulz)

To My Neighbour's Cat

Last night it snowed again.

Winter had its last laugh
at people who put away
winter boots and snow shovels.

But you're an outdoor cat.
Or, at least,
Doreen thinks so.

Do outdoor cats
glory in the machismo
of lying under my car
waiting until the last moment
before I start the engine?

I've seen your grey-and-white furball
sunning on Doreen's kitchen windowsill
as if you were waiting to be served a drink
on your own private beach.

Do outdoor cats
meow plaintively
under the canopy
outside my front door?

Last night it snowed again...

But you're an outdoor cat.
Or, at least,
Doreen thinks so.

Believe You're a Puppy and Other Advice from Echo

Accept compliments graciously. (They're all true, anyway.)

Keep nudging for treats.

<u>Rules for effective nudging</u>:
1. Gently touch your human with your nose.
2. Observe every time your human puts food on her fork. Watch the trajectory carefully. If it falls on the floor, it's yours!
3. If your human eats too neatly, put your head on her thigh and gaze adoringly at her. Works every time.

Eat each meal as if someone were going to take it away from you.

Keep nudging for treats.

Life is an eat-all-you-can buffet table.

Flowerbed fences provide a high-jumping challenge.

Guard the door from invasions by mail, newspapers and advertising flyers.

Chinese Food Delivery requires your utmost vigilance. Stay near the front door, in High Alert mode. The food could come at any time. Bark at any sound that might be a delivery car in the driveway. (You don't want it to get cold, do you?)

Keep nudging for treats.

Greet new dogs with a polite sniff, circle, leash tangle, and play invitation.

A well-timed burp is an excellent way to participate in human conversation.

Human "garbage" is often the tastiest of treats.

"Birthday" is a ridiculous human concept. Accept the praise and the extra treats, but otherwise, ignore it.

You're a puppy as long as you believe you're a puppy.

Always believe you're a puppy.

Dance with your leash.

Acknowledgements

I am grateful to the following people, all of whom had a role in helping me to produce this book. Huge thanks to:

My parents for their encouragement and support. If my father were alive, he'd foist a copy on each of you, waiting until you had read it in front of him. My mother and the antique baby grand piano which she gave us were inspirations for this book. After evaluating the type size of my name on the cover, she would have raved, and then said, "And how often do I rave?"

Gratitude and love to my patient, supportive, and funny husband, Michael Katz. As Dodo in *Animal Crackers* says, "Mere words cannot express my feelings."

My fabulous agent, Kris Rothstein.

My critique group, the Feathered Pens. Susan See, Kelly Barson, and Cana Rensberger helped me choose the title and encouraged me. The Warpies, my other writers' group. My writer buddies on LiveJournal and Blogger. I'm so lucky to have you all as friends.

My amazing cover designer, Kevin Slattery. Thank you for your imagination and humour.

Linda Everett and Adam Henry Carrière, the editors respectively of *Free Zone Quarterly* and *Danse Macabre*, who published many of these poems.

Readers of my website (http://barbaraetlin.com) and blog (http://owlsquill.blogspot.ca). You sent me my first fan letters.

Bouquets of parrot tulips to the special people who promised to buy a copy.

Linda M. Au, humour writer and expert proofreader. Thanks for fixing my formatting and tolerating my Canadianisms.

The woman at the 2004 Maui Writers' Conference who heard my poetry reading at Open Mic Night, took my ticket at the door two days later, and asked whether I had written a book of poetry. When I said, "No," she said, "You should."

You, the reader. Thank you. I hope you enjoy it.

ABOUT THE AUTHOR

Barbara Etlin's humorous poetry appeared in *Danse Macabre* and *Free Zone Quarterly*. Her profile of James Houston was a cover story in *enRoute*. Besides poetry and journalism, she writes novels for children. She lives in Toronto with one husband, one dog, two electronic cats, and about 300 owls. Please visit her website, http://barbaraetlin.com.

www.ingramcontent.com/pod-product-compliance
Lightning Source LLC
Chambersburg PA
CBHW051702040426
42446CB00009B/1254